How to be a...
Perfect
Princess

Contents

Chapter 1-Manners Matter
How To Behave Like a Princess

Chapter 2-Meeting and Greeting
How To Speak Like a Princess

Chapter 3-Dressing The Part
How To Dress Like a Princess

Chapter 4-Gliding, Curtseying, and Waving
How To Move Like a Princess

Chapter 5-Kissing Frogs
How To Find a Prince

Perfect Princess Quiz

Manners Matter

How to Behave like a Princess

Talking the Talk

A princess must always be charming and able to keep a conversation going, even if she is speaking to the most boring person in the room.

If you are in a receiving line, you probably won't have to say more than something like "lovely to meet you," however, it will be a different

matter if you are at a royal function.
Your conversation skills will be tested
a bit more and you'll have to have all your
princess talk talents at the ready.

It's always a good idea to read through the newspapers and
watch the news before a royal function so that you know
what's going on in the world. Always start a conversation by
asking someone a question about himself or herself. It will
get them talking and shows that you're interested in other
people. Don't talk about yourself unless someone asks you a
question - you don't want to be known as a conceited bore!
And NEVER talk about anyone else-you don't want to be
known as a gossip.

At a banquet, once you're seated, check to see who the queen
is speaking with-the person on her right or her left, and then
do the same. By time you get to the third or fourth course
in the meal, it's time to switch your attention to the person
on your other side. And NEVER speak to the person on the
other side of the table.

If you find there is an awkward pause in the conversation,
just ask another question, but make sure
it's not a personal question and that
the person is happy to answer it.

At Home (that would be the palace)

You may have more than one home: sometimes a royal family will have several—a summer one, a winter one, one in town, and one in the country. And it is a princess's responsibility to know her home (or homes) like the back of her hand—the sneaky back way to the kitchen for midnight snacks, the best banisters to slide down, and the hiding places no one else knows about. Although sneaking and hiding are great fun, ultimately you do need to be a picture-perfect princess when you're at home.

It's not easy to be a young girl, let alone a member of a royal family, and the higher your rank the more people will look to you to behave like a real lady. As a princess it is essential to remember these key points: Be polite to your family members—even little brothers, as they may someday be king. Be kind and considerate—remember to thank your staff for all the things they do for you; it takes

a lot to keep your life running smoothly! Be punctual—keeping people waiting might be OK for prima donna actresses and singers, but it's not acceptable for someone in your position.

And when you're at home, it's not all about sitting around
eating chocolates. You will need to write thank-you notes,
help organize charity events, have a riding lesson, etc., so
although you might be able to dress casually at
home, you will always have to be on your best
behavior. You might bump into tourists who
are taking a tour of the palace, so make sure
you smile, be gracious, and give a little royal wave.

Out and About

You need be picture-perfect at home, and you need to be even more so when you are out and about. The eyes of the world will be on you, and you need to make sure that you make your family–and your country–proud.

The rules of being polite, considerate, and punctual still apply when you are performing your royal duties outside the palace walls. So whether you're cutting a ribbon at a new hospital, having lunch at the Princess Guild, or attending a movie premiere, you need to be on your very best behavior.

Here are some tips that will help you get through those moments when everyone is checking out your manners, posture, smile, and graciousness:

- Remember to smile and wave to the entire crowd. Make everyone–even those people who are at the very back–feel as you've come especially to meet them.

- You may have to shake quite a lot of hands at an event, so wearing a pair of soft gloves will help you with all that meeting and greeting.

- If you will be standing for a long time, make sure you are wearing

comfortable shoes and keep your knees slightly bent.
This will stop your legs from getting too tired.

And create some secret signals that you can use with your
staff if you need a bit of help at an event. For instance, if you
rub your nose it means you've forgotten someone's name,
a cough from a lady-in-waiting means your tiara is slipping,
and if your chauffeur tugs on his ear it means that a prince
with sweaty palms is further down the receiving line.

Meeting and Greeting

How to Speak Like a Princess

With Your Public

A princess must always speak clearly and thoughtfully, and she must know how to use the English language (and hopefully speak some other languages as well). And when

you're out in public, everyone will be straining to hear your voice and how you speak.

Starting a conversation and keeping it going are a very important royal skill. It is important to start off a conversation with something other than "how are you" or "what do you do?" Everyone expects those questions, so if you start with a different question, it should pleasantly surprise the person to whom you are speaking and get the conversation going. Ask questions, but don't conduct an interview—there is a fine line between being interested and prying. And if you're meeting a lot of people, you need to make sure you spend just the right amount of time with each person.

Making a good impression when you meet and greet your public is also very important. You should never look as if you are trying too hard, and listening carefully goes hand-in-hand with asking questions and making conversation. Never let your eyes wander to someone or something that looks or sounds more interesting, even if a painting on the wall seems more riveting than the conversation you're trying to have.

Once you get to a certain age, you might be asked to make a speech at an event or an opening. It can be a bit nerve-wracking, but practice, practice, practice and it won't seem so scary.

With Your Staff

Not only do you need to speak like a princess when you are out and about, you also need to speak like a princess when you are at home. There may be an army of servants at your beck and call to make sure your life runs smoothly, however, you still need to treat them with respect.

The word to remember when dealing with your staff is manners, manners, manners. You need to speak politely to everyone—whether they are a plumber or one of your ladies-in-waiting. Make sure you learn the names of the people who work at the palace. Never raise your voice, yell at anyone, or lose your temper. And never gossip with or about any of your staff.

The staff who you will be have the most contact with are your ladies-in-waiting (who are hand-picked by the queen), and they will probably be your age. So they are kind of like BFFs and star servants rolled into one. But just because you will hang out with them, you still need to be polite and thoughtful. Your private secretary organizes your diary, helps you make decisions, gives you advice, and deals with the press for you. Therefore, you need to treat him with the utmost consideration and kindness, as he can stop you from

getting into sticky situations. Other staff who you will see around the palace are your dresser, maids, butlers, pages, and footmen.

And don't forget the kitchen staff! When there's been a banquet at the palace, be sure to thank all of them at the end of the evening. It might just get you a midnight snack to take back to your room.

At Events

You also need to speak like a true princess when you are at a banquet, a tea party, or any royal event–you never know who may be sitting or standing next to. A good thing to remember is to listen to whomever you're speaking with as if what they are saying is the most interesting thing in the world. Again, in these situations, listening is just as important as speaking.

When you are at event, it is OK for other royals to call you by your first name, but only until you're 18. After that, they may address you as Ma'am. Members of the public should address you

as "Your Royal Highness." And the same goes when you are addressing other royals. And the queen and king should be addressed as "Your Majesty."

Banquets are probably the most important social events you will be required to attend, and your speaking skills must be razor sharp. As a princess, you will be expected to speak with wit, charm, and always keep the conversation flowing. As soon as you receive the invitation, your staff will get a seating plan and will give you reports on the other guests so that you are sure you know what-and what not-to say.

After banquet is over, the queen will excuse herself and leave the room. All the women and girls should follow her out of the dining room. The men will stay behind. The ladies will retire to the drawing room, and this will be your chance to discuss the banquet and the dinner guests. But remember-no gossiping!

Dressing The Part

How to Dress like a Princess

Royal Fashion Rules

As a princess, you will be expected to be a fashion plate and trendsetter. You will most likely have ladies-in-waiting and a stylist to help you choose clothes, but you also need to have your own sense of style. Learn what looks good on you and which type of clothes work with your shape and size and which colors work with your hair color and skin tone. It will help if you have a natural flair for fashion, but that isn't as necessary as remembering these basic rules.

Buy good quality clothes; they may be a bit more expensive than the main stream shops, but you will get what you pay for and they will last longer. Make sure you have some classic pieces in your wardrobe and some of this season's trends.

Casual is OK, as long as you don't look scruffy or sloppy. You need to remember that the public will be looking at you all the time and that you will be photographed a lot, so you need to make sure you always look your best.

Dare to be different—always add your own personality to what you wear, as it will catch people's eye and reinforce that you are unique and have your own mind.

And make-up and hair are as important to the clothes you wear. Don't wear too much make-up you always need to look fresh-faced and clean. Keep your hair clean and the style simple (unless you're off to a ball). And make sure you change it regularly. It's good to give yourself a different look from time to time.

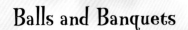

Balls and Banquets

On the days when you're not out cutting a ribbon at an opening or attending a banquet, it's acceptable to dress casually. But when you're at a royal function or out meeting your public, you need to look like a perfect princess. That doesn't mean you have to be decked out in a full-length gown, but you do need to look put-together and polished.

It's important that you feel confident and comfortable in whatever you're wearing before you leave the palace. Make sure you spend some time in front of a mirror and check your appearance from all angles. Also practice walking and sitting in whatever you've got on. You don't want to end up tripping on a hem or wobbling in your heels.

Here are some tips on what to wear to different occasions you may be required to attend:

- State occasions—Make sure you look sophisticated and stylish. A bit of fashion flair is OK, but you don't want to shock with whatever you're wearing.

- Walkabouts—Make sure you walk around in your outfit at home before you greet your public. You certainly don't want to be snapped by the paparazzi looking inappropriate.

- Foreign visits—This is your chance to shine, so take a selection of fantastic outfits and jewels to match. It's best to make as good an impression as possible when you're meeting diplomats and dignitaries.

And every perfect princess knows that beauty begins in the bathroom. Looking and smelling clean and fresh is the way to start every royal day—no matter what you're wearing!

Jewels, Jewels, Jewels!

Lots of girls dream of wearing a tiara, and unless you are a princess, a beauty pageant winner, or are getting married, you will never get a chance to wear one. But wait—you ARE a princess, so you'll have lots of opportunities to wear a tiara, as well as lots of other lovely jewelry!

Young princesses are usually expected to wear only pearls, but as you grow up you can start to dig deeper into the family jewelry box, and your mother will hopefully pass down her heirloom jewelry to you.

One basic rule to remember is that you can either wear large earrings or an extravagant necklace, but not together. You want to avoid looking like a Christmas tree. However, when you're not in public and are in the privacy of your own room, you can certainly try on all your jewelry at one time!

In some countries, royal rules state that a princess can't wear a tiara until after she's married, but that rule doesn't apply in every. In countries where princesses aren't allowed to wear tiaras until they're married, unmarried princesses may have half-tiaras, which are like hairbands with a jewel in the middle.

Your jewelry can be heavy, so you will need to practice wearing it. Have one of your ladies-in-waiting help you put on the jewelry and practice walking up and down a palace hallway. And it's also a good idea to practice making sure your earrings, necklaces, bracelets, and rings don't get tangled in your hair or snag your clothing. With a bit of practice, you'll be a perfect bejewelled princess!

How to Move Like a Princess

Gliding—down stairs, across the floor, into a chair

Just as important as behaving, speaking, and dressing like a princess is moving like a princess. You will be expected to be elegant and graceful, and your every move will be scrutinized whether you're attending a state banquet, at a movie premiere, or having dinner at home with your parents.

You will most likely be given deportment (a fancy word for how to behave and conduct yourself) lessons. One of the hardest lessons you'll have to master is how to move in a long gown. Push your right toe gently forward and take a step, bring your left toe forward in the same way. Let the gown trail behind you a little. The trick is to try and walk from your knees down rather than from your thighs and hips. This might sounds a bit strange, but if you walk this way it keeps your body still and makes it looks as if you're gliding.

You will also have to walk down lots of flights of stairs with people watching you. This will be tricky since you shouldn't

look down! Instead you should look out and smile at the people who are watching you The best way to do this is to go slowly while gently holding onto the banister. And if you can quickly count how many steps there are before you start down–it will be a breeze!

When you go to sit down in a chair, lower yourself slowly into the chair rather than collapsing into it. Keep your back straight, your knees together, and your hands folded in your lap. You can cross your legs, but only at the ankles. You may need to sit for several hours, so be prepared!

The Perfect Curtsey

The word curtsey comes from "courtesy," and it is a respectful bow to someone that you're meeting. But as a princess, you only have to curtsey to people who are more important than you—which is hardly anyone!

So here's how to perform the perfect curtsey: Put your weight onto your left foot and then position your right foot behind your left heel. Set your right toe down and bend both knees as you slowly lower yourself. The trick is move smoothly down while keeping your body upright and tilting your head just a little. Then look up with a smile and extend your right hand for the person your curtseying to.

For a quick curtsey, just put your right foot behind your left leg and bend your knees while holding your skirt or dress out to the side

A princess will be expected to curtsey to foreign royal families as well. In these situations, it is best to hold out your skirt and raise your right hand to be kissed. As well as curtseying when you're introduced to a member of a royal family, you should also curtsey when they leave the room.

Some etiquette professionals say that nowadays it really isn't necessary to curtsey to members of the royal family,

but since it is a sign of respect, it is still a good idea to curtsey when you have the opportunity.

These days in some situations it will acceptable to shake hands rather than curtsey when you meet a member of the royal family or when people are meeting you. So while you need should be ready to receive or give a curtsey, you should also be prepared to shake hands at events–so always have a pair of gloves with you!

The Royal Wave

There is a special style and certain way
to wave like a royal. But every member
of the royal family has a different method of waving,
and your wave will become your trademark. You should
start practicing at an early age, and you should make sure
you've mastered it by the time you make your first official
appearance in front of the public.

When you have to wave to your public it shouldn't be
over-the-top. The secret to a perfect princess wave is all in
the wrist. A subtle twist of the wrist will give you that "oh
so royal wave," and it will save your energy while waving
for what might be hours on end as a parade passes by.

There have been a lot of super wavers in royal families
around the world. Queen Elizabeth II of England has
perfected the twist of the wrist so that her wave is just a
small movement of her hand. She also holds her forearm
in a right angle and her hand is slightly clenched with her
fingers together. The queen then rotates the wrist in a
slow and regal manner.

Princess Alexandra of Denmark uses the flat palm
technique—she raises her arm and keeps her palm facing out
to her subjects.

Princess Mary of Denmark is a very keen waver and she uses her whole arm—from fingertip to shoulder—when she waves. (It must make her very tired!)

Princess Grace of Monaco used the elbow only method, which she did by moving the forearm in a windshield wiper motion.

So get practicing that pretty little princess wave that you will become known for!

Kissing Frogs

How to Find a Prince

Where to Look

In days gone by, finding a prince wasn't a problem. Your parents would have known lots of other royal families, and they would most likely have arranged a marriage for you. However, these days a princess pretty much has to look

for her own prince, but at least you won't get stuck with someone who is a bit sweaty or smells funny.

You'll have lots of opportunities to seek out your prince, and there will be lots of places to look for him. You will go to lots of balls, polo matches, ballets, etc., and there should be available princes at most of these events. However, although you are a confident princess, it's always best for someone else to make the introduction. And you need to make sure that the introduction is made properly and according to the customs of your country.

You will also be traveling and you'll get to meet royalty from around the world, so you might meet a prince in an exotic location. Long-distance relationships can be a bit tough, but if you find a prince halfway around the world, you can make it work these days since phone, email, and long-distance travel make keeping in touch a lot easier than in it was 400 years ago!

Your family is also key in helping you find a prince. They will put out feelers for eligible princes around the world. You won't necessarily need to marry a prince, but it will be best if you marry some kind of royalty, so if he's not a prince, he should be a duke, a marquess, an earl, or a viscount.

Picking a Prince

You might find that you have a lot of suitors—after all, you are a perfect princess! Not all of them will be to your liking and you will have to "kiss a lot of frogs" before you find your Prince Charming. Don't worry if it takes some time—your Prince Charming is out there!

It's important to remember that some princes are actually in disguise, probably as a result of an evil spell. The most common disguise is that of a frog prince. So if you've found a frog you might think is actually a promising prince in disguise, you might just have to kiss him, as kissing a frog prince is the only way to break the spell. But make sure that you aren't just kissing a common frog—or worse yet—a warty toad!

Other princes have been disguised as beasts or ogres. Breaking the spell that keeps them in this state is a bigger matter than just a kiss, and you have to prove your love for them even though they are ugly, smell bad, and growl. (Think *Beauty and the Beast*.)

The best plan is to avoid princes that are disguised as frogs or ugly beasts and look for a prince who is already in human form. It may take some time to find him, and when you do he should be kind, considerate, honest, trustworthy, interested in and devoted to you, make you laugh, and like your friends and family. Again, it may take you a while to find a prince that ticks most of these boxes, but hang in there.

Happily ever after is possible!

Passing the Test

So you may have found your Prince Charming, however, he may want to check that you're a real princess before you head down the aisle. If that's the case, you will need to pass the Princess and the Pea test. This test involves being able to feel a tiny pea under a stack of mattresses. Now this can be a bit tricky and some princes might make it more difficult by using a mushy pea that is impossible to feel under all those mattresses. Hopefully your prince won't be tricky with you, and you will actually feel the pea. However, the test is based on a fairy tale, so it's hard to say whether or not any princess has ever really felt that pea under all those mattresses. So the best thing to do is to in the morning tell the prince that you didn't get a wink of sleep. This will prove to him that you are in fact a true, perfect princess and hopefully he will get down on one knee and ask you to marry him.

Hopefully there will be a Royal Wedding once you've found your Prince Charming, he's passed your tests, and you've passed his. There will be lots of things to plan, cakes to taste, flowers to choose, and best of all—a wedding dress to choose. Of course there will be plenty of time to arrange everything, and you will have a lot of help to pull the plans together and make the wedding day a huge success.

Just remember to enjoy it all and then you can head off into your Happily Ever After with your Prince Charming!

Perfect Princess Quiz

Take this quiz to see if you are a real perfect princess:

1. Your father (the king) marries again and your stepmother and her daughters are mean to you. Do you:

    A. Sit in a corner and cry?
    B. Put dirt in their dinner?
    C. Try to be kind to them?

2. A frog wearing a small crown jumps in your lap while you're reading in the garden. Do you:

    A. Run away screaming?
    B. Throw it back in the pond?
    C. Give it a kiss, as it may be a prince in disguise?

3. You trip slightly while making an entrance down the stairs to a ball. Do you:

    A. Burst into tears and run back up the stairs?
    B. Apologize to everyone and walk down the rest of the staircase hanging your head?
    C. Stop for a moment, put a smile on your face, and keep walking with your head held high?

4. You are seated next to a rather boring, elderly man at a banquet. Do you:

    A. Cover your mouth as you yawn all the time he's talking to you?
    B. Try to ignore him and speak to the person on the other side of you?
    C. Listen to what he's saying as if it's the most important thing in the world?

If you answered:
    Mostly As - Did you read this book?
    Mostly Bs - You need to get in touch with your inner princess a bit more.
    Mostly Cs - Congratulations! You are a perfect princess!